HEAVENLY

FROM ABOVE

God, thank you for the beautiful gift which you have given.

May this book help others to grow closer to you!

HEAVENLY MESSAGES FROM ABOVE

A Practical Guide to Handling Life's Challenges and Finding Your Inner Peace and Truth

CATHERINE PAGANO

Published by: ADVANTAGE BOOKS™
                  www.advbookstore.com

Library of Congress Catalog Number: 2021945027

Name:	Pagano, Catherine, Author
Title:	Heavenly Messages From Above / Catherine Pagano
Description	Longwood: Advantage Books, 2021
Identifiers:	(print): 9781597556606
	(epub): 9781597556721
Subjects:	RELIGION: Christian Life - Inspirational

First Printing: December 2021
21 22 23 24 25 26   10 9 8 7 6 5 4 3 2 1

Table of Contents

INTRODUCTION

Spirit of God- Guide me
Grace of God- Protect me
Will of God- Mold me
Love of God- Be always with me

How difficult is it for humans to follow this? Merging your Free Will with the Will of God is very hard for so many. The craziness of this world today has lured, pushed, and pulled many people away from God. What really is one's true center? Confused by the high pace of activity, people are bombarded by negativity and are unable to handle it. This book will hopefully guide those that wish to come back to the peaceful center that each person longs for on a daily basis.

The book is a guide. You must understand that the success you have is dependent on the effort you put in to make it- the more effort- the more success.

A basic premise of this book is that Life is a Journey. You are not alone as move on this path and most importantly we are here to assist you. In truth, we wish you many blessings along the way.

Yet Dear One, each day we observe the great struggles humans have with time. There is never enough so they say. But that is not true! Each moment, each second as they move forward is a chance to make things right. No matter what it might be.

Yet for humans, it is wasted on the negative or the mundane, instead of using it to make something good or positive. Then at the end of the day humans think that the day passed so quickly but what did I accomplish. How strange that is to us.

Take a different perspective. Time is a variable that moves. Humans move through it. Why? So change can take place. A new opportunity is in every moment, every second. Welcome it! Enjoy it! Use It!

Think of it like a journey. A journey for your growth. Time is vehicle so that you may move forward on to the things you need to get to in your life. The things you are supposed to learn in this life comes in stages. Perhaps you would consider it as an unfolding of ideas each in its own divine timing.

If you welcome time as the means by which you learn and grow; then you come to understand the patterns that are in your life. From this you can see where you have come from; but more importantly the things you need to work on as you move forward.

It is those things that you must focus on. For in truth, whatever has passed is gone. So, no need to hold on to it. That is the beauty of time. In a human way, each day is a "do over" every day. Till you get it and then you move on to your next stage or thing you need to work on. If you think about it- why this moment called the present. So, you can give a gift to yourself by learning what you need to learn. Or even better yet by giving something to someone else to help them on their journey through time.

It is truly a very intricate web that you are a part of in this life. The key for you is to understand it more fully so you can make the most of each day and enjoy the time you have.... For it is an incredible journey. We love you and are always with you.

Chapter 1

It begins…

The most interesting thing about life is just to begin. For many they go through life by just existing- They do little, say little, and have little-yet-they want it all. How funny!

They look to GOD and everyone else to do it for them. THAT IS NOT HOW IT WORKS! The key is just to begin. BEGIN LIFE- BEGIN LIVING- How?

Just start with each day- no more no less- Consider the gift of each day as a box that you are to fill with good ideas, actions and deeds completed. Some days you might feel that you filled the box till it is overflowing and others you might feel think that you did not.

It is not to be measured in human terms but in GOD'S eyes. The key is to just begin leaving no day with an empty box. Each day matters- just begin- That is your task- your mission.

Let kind words and deeds for others become your goal and before you know it you will see and feel the positive energy move through you.

It will bring you to new heights. You will release the old negative thoughts and hurts. You will start to care more about others than yourself. It will help you to heal and grow in such a smooth easy way that you will not even realize how you are being transformed into one of GOD'S beautiful angels on earth.

It is in each of us. It is GOD'S hope for us in this life- The key is just to begin.

Be still and know that I am.

Chapter 2

Assessing Your Life's Journey

Why is it so difficult for humans to trust God?

They would rather put their trust in the newspaper, weatherman or an investor than God? How strange!

God is the alpha and the omega, the beginning and the end. The "ALL KNOWING"- So why not trust HIM? What are humans so afraid of?

Because they cannot see God-they do not believe that He truly exists. What little faith! This book is to help you have faith- To teach you to trust.

Have God enter into your life- So you will be a trusting, loving being. The exact way God intended you to be.

Throughout time humans have repeated the same mistakes. It is almost funny. The first fear we see is that they fear love.

This is ridiculous! Why not embrace it?

For what is love? Love is the BEST human feeling possible. It makes people feel whole. It gives comfort. It shows caring for another is rewarding.

When you give- you get back. It teaches that one person cannot survive in a good quality manner- alone.

To so many, it is bad because it makes you vulnerable and weak. How crazy! You are already THAT!

It is love that protects you from the weakness.

You are human- made by GOD- Of Course, You are vulnerable and weak! That is the way you were made.

But GOD gives you LOVE to make you strong. Showing you to do the same for other humans, thus making you even stronger yet. So IT IS LOVE THAT MAKES YOU STRONG!

Get it? We still cannot figure out- why most humans do not!

Facing Life's Daily Challenges....

A person's lifetime is meant to challenge them, so he or she can grow and evolve to higher levels of thinking. It is not intended to get stuck in the "same old, same old"!

We find it interesting that this "same old, same old" concept is very popular in American culture today. How often do you hear a person reply when asked- What's new?

"Oh, nothing- same old, same old."

What a shame! GOD gives each person a "new day"- each and every day they live!

Why? So- they can make new and different choices. Make changes. Try new things. Experience life and grow. Evolve to new heights. Correct behavior from the past. Begin again!

So why has human thinking allowed he or she to get "stuck" in the same old, same old logic! Begin again.... Change this concept.

Treat each day as precious. A new chance to start over. A chance to grow... A chance to love... A chance to make a difference... You can you know.

Just begin with a new attitude for TODAY and watch what happens. Each day is a new day to begin. Write a new script for your life NOW!

Each new day... a new beginning!

Finding Your Purpose....

It is important to realize that everyone has a purpose. Their very own mission, which was selected or chosen depending on how you look at it- just for them.

There is most definitely a divine plan. Each person has a part to play in this divine plan. Unfortunately- everyone has free will. This thing called "free will" can alter the plan if one is not careful. So you might say- well why would a person want to choose to alter the divine plan?

Fear, Ego, Lack of understanding, Lack of love, Lack of trust.

The divine plan brings out the higher good in a person. Truly shows them what they are capable of doing. But some people fear that.

These very pages are and have been written as part of the divine plan, so that YOU can learn and make the conscious choice to follow the Divine Plan.

There are NO COINCIDENCES!

You are here right now reading these words because you need to be reminded of YOUR PURPOSE, the very reason of why you exist and the very important understanding that you need to follow your mission, your purpose in this Divine Plan.

A Challenge?

Yes!

A Reminder?

Yes!

Now – Put aside any fear, ego, or negative thought, and let us get going on the road to your purpose. A very rewarding journey indeed.

What determines your Happiness?

Is it a person's actions, the day of the week, the weather, a good meal, a kind word…. The list could go on and on…

But did you notice – all of the "things" we listed here are external. What that means is they are outside the control of one person. In fact, they might even involve another person. Right from that would be a human's misconception.

NO HAPPINESS---- NO "TRUE" HAPPINESS CAN BE FOUND THIS WAY.

True Happiness comes from within. Inside a person- It is either there or it is not! If it is not the person must ask themselves two questions:

One: WHY NOT?

Two: DO I WANT TO BE HAPPY?

Regarding #1: Why not? Why not –ask? What is it that is stopping you? God is not in the way here. God is not punishing you here- you are.

God created you happy. Your mind, Your ego, in all that has happened to you has developed anger, fear, guilt, ideas of punishment, and then your mind allowed all of this to take over. Making each day a battle with every word or action by you or others. Completely stopping any form of happiness from entering in.

In fact – we think humans call it by a most ridiculous expression- Life sucks.

DO YOU HAVE ANY IDEA OF HOW BIZARRE THAT IS? LIFE DOES NOT SUCK, HUMANS DO!

Learn to connect with the Divine and we will truly show you.

On the second question- Do I want to be happy? NOW, we ask you- DO YOU? If the answer is even slightly –yes, We applaud you! Because your inner voice, no matter how fragile, is crying out "free me". Free you- you might ask? Well it means that all of the worst of negative thinking has weighed you down to the point that your inner spirit is overburdened. Lighten up! Remove those shackles. Release the inner spirit and fly free.

It is the way you were intended. Now this does not means no responsibility to you or loved ones. It means release all actions in life as a burden, duty, or obligation requiring a response or control. Release it all and "DO" because it the right thing to do.

A simple rule which cleans it all up- Do anything and everything because it is the right thing to do! From just that all WILL change. Life will be better because you will be more centered and the more centered you are the more happiness enters and lives within you. It really is very simple. Please do not complicate it with human ways- Just try it.

Live, Love, and be happy! It is the way you have been created. Peace!

Step by step the pages of this book will guide you to new and higher levels of thinking to keep you on your divine path.

So allow us to let the journey unfold. Allow us to lead you to a life even better than you have ever dreamed of… because it is part of the divine plan. It is why you are here… Let us begin.

Step 1- Examine Your Thoughts

Did you ever stop to "think" how many thoughts go through your mind each day? It is truly amazing! So, there are days you are amazed and other days you wish "they" would stop. You do not want to even think.

But you cannot stop thinking…. So what do you think about? Start anywhere or time you like.

Keep a record of your thoughts for any one given day. List it in whatever topic form you feel comfortable. Try to put your thoughts on a blank paper. Then make your list as you go through the day.

The best way to do this is to start when you get up. First list any dreams you remember from that night. Then as you go through the day what thoughts enter your mind. List them as they occur or soon after especially if you are dwelling on them or if some thoughts keep coming back.

Just list them in the order they occur. If you were to go back after several hours you will lose quite a few. So try to set aside a day when you can devote to yourself to do this.

The more you do this earnestly the greater the reward at the end. We understand if your life is so busy that you cannot do this for a whole day. But try to do this for as long as you can. You will get to the point of it if you do this earnestly.

Once the day is over... examine your list of thoughts.Separate them into categories. First like this-

- Positive or Negative Thoughts (or Emotions)

- On people or ideas or yourself

- Creative ideas or same ideas

- Happy thoughts or sad or indifferent ones

- After you categorize them.

- What have you noticed about thoughts?

- What does your thoughts tell you about you?

- What were you feeling as these thoughts were on your mind?

Be analytical here. The more the better. It helps later. What have you learned? As you examine your thoughts what did you learn about yourself?

How much of your thinking is spent on... Worrying? Anger? Re-hashing ideas over and over again? Frustration? Questions unanswered? Negative ideas?

How much of your thinking is spent on... Being creative... Ideas to help another human? Ideas to improve your quality of life or the lives of others? Seeking knowledge for knowledge sake? Loving ideas? Positive ideas?

Where are you? What are you thinking about the most?

Remember- you are what you think! If your thoughts are primarily in the negative column, any wonder why you do not feel good?

Each negative thought releases toxins into your body over time these toxins build up in the parts of the body directly related to your thinking. Eventually ill health "dis-ease" will develop. Honestly, how could it not? So, remember you must realize your thoughts are very, very powerful to you and your body.

On the other hand, positive thoughts release healing energy into your body--- releasing and purifying any toxins.

We could never understand why humans would choose to stay negative when there is so much more to be said for the POSITIVE. That is why we are sending this message to you today.

WAKE UP---- Change your thinking!

Work on being more positive. Nothing is by coincidence- remember you need to hear this NOW that is why you are here now reading this. The path is clear- using your free will make the right choice. Think Positive! All else will follow......Try it ...see... what happens.

The next step is to examine your daily behavior.

Humans always think about things before they do them. True but there are times when they have thought about things and then go do another. So since we have asked you to examine your thoughts. We now ask you to examine your actions.

Using the same concept. At the end of any given day- examine what you have done for the day.

Have you actions been positive? Negative? Have you tried to help others? How much of your day is spent in each of these?

Did you accomplish anything today? How much would you categorize what you did as Positive? Negative?

Do you feel satisfied with yourself based on what you did with the day? What would you do differently?

Take the time to really answer these questions. Write down as much as possible. Then go to sleep.

During the next day examine what you wrote. Consider yourself. Look at what you are and have done? Are you happy with you? Where would you make changes no matter how small? What suggestions do you have for yourself? Write it all down.

Focus on the positive ways you can improve. All humans can improve! Concentrate on that. Make a plan of ways you can help yourself improve. In the next step we will show you how to make this plan work! Are still with us….

If this is getting too hard – put it down wait three days and try again.

Above all don't get discouraged just keep trying again until you get past this.

We want you to succeed and will help you. The key is you have to want to succeed too. Patience. The divine plan is working…

Step 2- Learning to Adapt to Change

Humans are funny- they say they want change but rarely act to produce it. This chapter will focus on the tools a person can use to give them change in their lives.

Let's start with the topic of change itself. What is change? Humans understand it to be some act or thing which alters the life they have known. Usually, it implies making a different routine or making a difference. Change is usually or often times viewed with fear, hesitancy, or in trepidation. WHY?

Change is a vital part of life. So why try to hold on to something? Let it GO. Go with the flow of energy to see where it lands you. To say the least this is probably one of the hardest things for humans to do. WHY? Let's take a moment to explore the human psyche.

Humans are a creature of habit. They like things the same. It makes or gives comfort to a human knowing that everything is the same. "Same old, same old" How ridiculous!

Nothing is the same. Each second gives forth new life and ends life. The body naturally replaces cells while discarding the old cells. A human thought passes through the body thus altering the vibration from before. So why fear change? Welcome it as a natural part of life!

Your attitude on this will make all the difference here. Granted some things are easy to apply to this; while some things are far too difficult to humanly give up that easy. Words like "I can't", "I don't know how", "Why", "What will happen to me" and "I'm afraid" all enter in. To a human these are very real feelings to us they are not. Perhaps if we explain why they are not, humans might be able to find a way to adjust their attitudes.

We ourselves are "beings of light"- light which is an energy force. Together we are all of the same energy force. We flow in tandem to each other. If we were try to stop or impede this force we would alter all the energy force together. It would not be able to flow in the manner it was designed to by GOD. So we do not even think of trying.

Humans, however, do not see themselves as an energy force working in connection to the universal energy force. They see themselves as individuals and in most instances, they do not even see themselves as beings of light. So how could they impede all the energy force much less the divine plan of GOD? Humans underestimate their true power.

Once humans understand exactly what they are. The difference in their lives be astonishing! Getting them to understand this is the hard part.

It is why we are here explaining this and why (at least one reason) why you are here reading this now. So, you can see now why we say attitude makes all the difference.

Now ask yourself- what is your attitude? If you understand and believe what we are saying here, YOU are ready to begin the changes you want in your life. If you do not, digest what we have said---think---ponder----and when you are ready begin.

Now on to the plan.

Chapter 3

The PLAN

Humans always think the divine plan is cast in stone.

That really is not true. It is a vibrant, moving, constantly changing plan. Full of energy!

Humans do have free will. They always have choices, which alter the divine plan all the time.

The very notion that humans have influence over the divine plan is very difficult for the human population to swallow. Humans think that they are powerless. Not so! They do have power. Not complete Power but some. The one of the purposes behind these writings are to get humans to act more responsibly using the power they do have.

Humans do not use their powers wisely if at all. It is a common human condition to have the following:

When experiencing difficulties in life to wait for someone or something to come and fix it all. Make it all better. Have you ever done this? Why? Why would you expect another human to fix what you have created for yourself?

Now that question triggers a reaction –we are sure.

There two parts to that remark. One is that you, a human being, would expect another to help you. And the second is that you created the mess you are in. We have to laugh here. Because we are not sure which part humans have more trouble with- The First? Or the Second? We want to take a moment to discuss both.

Would you expect another human being to help you? How often do humans think that another person would? Or better yet should?

Most humans without a doubt go through life not only expecting people to help but demanding it. Why?

Where are you in all of this? Take a long hard look at how much you do expect from others. Do you think that it is required for them to help you? Do you expect more from one person than another and why? How do you react when you get what you want from them? What about when you do not? These questions are designed to get you to think about the extent you deliberately expect others to help you. So do you?

If the answer is yes- which we figure it would be, then we want you to consider honestly the following comments: Humans have weaknesses so why would rely on humans to help you and not God? It never ceases to amazes us on humans will but such trust in other humans when they know that at times disappointment will result. Yet, If you ask humans to put complete trust in God? They are skeptically. They suggest a series of what if thoughts or questions.

I am only human how could I possibly feel God wants to help me. What if God doesn't want me to do or say or have this or that? What if God really is upset with me for doing this or that? What if God says no? What if God gets angry at me?

And so on and so on. You get the drift.

How ridiculous! God is not about judgment or restriction. God is not about anger. God is not about punishment.

GOD is about LOVE!

A love that is so unconditional that humans really cannot understand completely. God loves you, as you are with no restrictions or judgments. God knows you make mistakes. You are human. He made you that way, so you could learn from your mistakes.

So, with that in mind why not learn to trust in God? Learn to develop your own personal relationship with Him. It is not as hard as you think. What is harder is relying on humans because at times you will frustrate yourself more than you realize.

Did you ever stop to think why you are reading this book now? Remember nothing is by coincidence. We will help you here.

You are reading this book and have gotten to this particular page because you want changes in your life. You want to make your life better and because you need ideas to help you make your plan for the rest of your life.

Otherwise you would be reading something else. You are ready. We know it. Now you do too.

Before we can begin we must still look at the second part to the earlier question. You ask which one? There are so many that we have thrown at you.

The part we would like to discuss is the fact that you are the creator of all the situations you are in. You can and do create the situations you find yourself in all the time. Humans have a hard time realizing this. How many times you hear people say….

I don't know why this is happening to me? Why me, what have I ever done? I know that God hates me because look at how He is punishing me with this?

So and so doesn't like me that why they treat me this way?

I can never …..

I should have done ….

I wish I was like this……

I would like to…..but…….

Sound familiar. Humans really are funny this way. STOP. THINK. LISTEN to yourselves.

God created you in His likeness. You possess more power than you are giving yourself credit for. You can influence what happens in your life.

Every situation you are in within your lifetime is directly shaped by how YOU act. Others will only respond to you based on the energy that YOU send out in the first place.

The depth and level to which YOU display love as opposed to negative energy means all the difference in the world. You then have influence over what happens to you!

Get it! Got it! Good!

A typical example might be the following: Humans spent a good portion of their lives looking for the "perfect mate". As they go through relationship after relationship, they develop the opinion no such person exists. Therefore, they must settle for whatever they are in at the moment. Not true.

Upon further examination, we see that each person walks in to each relationship with a set of preconceived ideas and images. For example, some people want this new love to be the "magical doctor". This means they want this new mate to magical transform their lives into something so special and perfect. They expect this new love to take away all the previous pain from other relationships by magically making it all better.

They want desperately to believe that this new love will cure all this ills of their lives. They expect this new love to instantly know all their own faults and failings. And hope that they will show them how to correct it all.

Those are pretty BIG demands and limitations this person is putting on another. Is there any wonder that the relationship fails?

In addition, they expect another to come into the relationship with no background baggage of their own. They are supposed to be a "New" individual with complete understanding, patience and no problems. Do you realize how ridiculous this is?

Individuals are brought together to learn from each other. In a way, it is like to rough stone that when rubbed together polish each other. Once they polish each other to their finished level, they move on. Yes, this is saying not all relationships are meant to last forever. Only romance novels could expect forever.

This is not to say there are not soulmates. Soulmates do exist. Individual souls who reconnect from previous lives that know each other so well and really feel like two halves of a whole. In the course of every human's evolution, which takes place across many lifetimes, every individual will experience a soulmate relationship once. Some are lucky enough to even have it more that once. We realize that this is much to ask you to accept, but here you must trust us on this. We also realize that depending on your own experience, level of perception and willingness to understand, this will or will not make great sense to you.

Now, let us get back to your expectations for a relationship. If you walk into a relationship with a preconceived fear that you will be hurt, then you will. If your ideas are that you are an enabler, constantly allowing a person to mistreat you because they "really do not mean it", then they will. If you want so much to control another person's behavior to the extent of what, when, and how they do something, then you will attract a person who will allow that done to them, even if it is only for a little while. If you walk into a relationship desiring and acting like you want a life partner, you will attract such a person.

Are you getting the picture now? Think about all your relationships in your life. Now apply what we have given you. Can you see how this works now? Yes it is a harsh admission to accept. But you do have a responsibility in every relationship for what you are doing. What you do automatically triggers a response in the other person. Based on how you present yourself automatically limits the response you get. Thus, the parameters of the relationship are limited. Thereby, causing the type of relationship you get. Over period of time, you can get stuck in situations, which can be so limiting that you are blinded to truth. And the truth is-you do have the power to change it all simply by changing you and your behavior. Now that sound simply and it really is but to humans it can be very hard.

What makes it hard is the inability of a human to change. The fear of change can immobilize a person to the point that they are paralyzed to all positive change. So they keep repeating the same mistakes but in different forms. So when they end up with the same behavior, their response is- I knew it would not work, I keep trying and it still fails.

Well, you are asking what can a human do? Think, act and be LOVE.

Love is the greatest gift if given unconditionally. Now we know you are shaking your heads and saying- Right If I give love, it will all work out. Sure!

I have done that, and know what, it did not work!

Well the key here is the unconditionally part. We know you have tried to do this but where you get stuck is directly related to the real meaning of unconditional. So we are going to help to "Lighten" up on this.

Unconditional means with no judgments, demands or complications. Remember this expression—"love given freely always without any strings will always be better that love given with any one or more conditions."

How many times humans will say- I love you but…. That is not love then that is caring for someone so long as they do what you want. What is wrong with that picture we ask you? If you don't know that answer stop reading the book- find the answer and come back to us, because you are stuck here.

Unconditional love allows each person to be who they need to be, grow and find their own true path for their own higher "good". Yet for some reason, humans are afraid of this. In a way what they fear is if the person is allowed to be who they are, they will then choose not to be that human's partner. With all due respect here- if this were to happen- why would you want to hold them back or force them to stay if it was not in their best interest?

Humans' lives are journeys into developing their higher good. The people one comes in contact with along the way are there to help us grow and develop. As we stated earlier, each relationship helps the persons involved to polish themselves. To become a better human, learn about oneself and evolve. If that has been accomplished between two people then it is time for them to move on. You have no right to hold them back.

This all seems difficult for a human because it involves change. And we all know how humans react to change. But with a little strength and perseverance, it is possible. That is why we are here to help humans figure this all out.

As we continue you will hear us speak to your inner being, the real you. The "you" that knows truth and love and wants so much to build that in your life. Moving forward to achieve that is not easy but the real you wants so much to get you moving that it will only take a little to get the ball rolling. After that, the more you follow the real you the better you will like your life. You see the real you knows the truth and is in tune with your divine plan, the plan that was meant for you. These thoughts alone should bring you much comfort. You see you are being guided. Never think that you are out there on your own alone. Ridiculous!

As we move on let us focus now on your plan.

Much time and consideration needs to be devote to what your thoughts and desires reflect as well as what your inner you is feeling. Think about experiences in your life in the past when you knew that you were doing what you needed to do. Your gut told so and within every aspect of your being it felt right. Remember those experiences....

Now what would you say if we told you could have that feeling all the time. Pretty amazing, is it not? You can.

Very often we are asked by humans- What am I supposed to do? What is my purpose here?

Each time we try to share some insight to each human being about their specific purpose. Some understand us while some do not. We realize that it is not a simple thing to understand. And we know the difficulty of trying to write these words to apply to all of you that read it. For this we return to a statement we made earlier. Your divine plan rests on the love you give to others. For it is in loving others that you show your love to God.

Each person was created with a special gift, a gift that is his or hers alone to give to the world. That gift may be to utilize throughout the person's lifetime, or it may be to use at one given moment or select moments in time. This much we can tell you. As to what your specific gift is, we ask you to speak to us privately in your heart and there you will find the answer. Just remember you must trust what you hear us speak and believe.

Thus, your life should center on your gift and you making conscious choices which reflect your understanding of your purpose. Your free will can keep you close to your purpose or get you far off track from the true purpose that you are to serve. To say the least, this can be very difficult for some humans. At this time, we expect that you are thinking about your life and just how much you are on track. So we thought it would be a great time to do a little self-analysis. We know you will find this helpful.

Think a few moments on what you think your gift is. If you need to write the thought down for future reference, please feel free to do so. For many people seeing your thought in writing is very helpful. As you write be honest with yourself. What do you think your gift is? How have you used your gift? Have you helped others or have used your gift to just benefit yourself or your immediate close relationships? Really think here. Trust what you are feeling and tell us honestly. Remember we have been with you always. So to lie to us is really rather stupid! We have seen you in every moment of your life. So who are you really kidding?

Now for those of you who are not sure of what your gift really is? We suggest the following: Give yourself a period of quiet time for reflection. Think about what you do best. If you still are not sure think about what people have complimented you on. Trust what you are feeling here and then ask yourself have you used this talent to help others or just yourself. This will bring you to where you need to be in order to continue.

Once you have done this, you are ready for the next step, the creation of your plan.

The plan we speak about is your effort to stay on track to what God has in mind for you.

As we stated before you have a direct influence in the operation of your divine plan so long as you remain a human. In order to make your plan you must first commit yourself to the fulfillment of it. Now right away some of you get nervous because you question the word commitment. The basis of your plan is commitment. You must honestly say and feel that you will do all in your power to try to stay on track to what you promise. We will not dwell on this need for commitment here but hope to shed some light on it in a later chapter. So for now let us move on.

Your commitment is simple. Make a daily resolve that you will do your best to follow this: Not my will Lord but thine be done! That each day you will make every effort to follow the Lord's will and not your own. After you commit to this you will find each day easier to handle. Because it will not be forcing what you think should happen, but the Lord's will for you. Remember- the Lord's knowledge is infinite and yours is limited. So why not let the Lord into your life- He does know better as to what is right for you. He created you!

When you think about this approach, it takes a tremendous amount of pressure off you. Think about how much time you spend worrying about what or how you should do something. What a waste of energy! With this resolve, you can free yourself up to just be a vehicle for God's light in you. This way you become free to work the miracles you were destined. Then you do in fact become very God like in your behavior. This is not to say you are God. You are just His vehicle on earth. Then suddenly you feel connected to the universe. Thus ending any fear of being alone and reinforcing the idea that you are never alone. All of this is very comforting to humans.

Now you are ready to make your plan- Here it is- think very simply here. I will to thy will. I WILL TO THY WILL... I WILL TO THY WILL... Then trust everything that follows. See how simple it is! Your plan is an ongoing work in process just like you. You cannot structure it to death and require it to follow through exactly. Remember life is a continuous journey of constant energy motion thus change is always possible. So why complicate it. Leave it open to divine intervention. Thus freeing you and others up to the greatest good for all. In a way the rule of thumb known as the greatest plan is no plan is partially true. Do not plan and structure your life to the point that there is no room for the acceptance of change. Leave it open and free to new ideas and adjustments. This is not to say that there is no plan. THERE MOST DEFINITELY IS! It is GOD'S PLAN. Not yours that should work in your life. You do not need or are able to understand all the interconnections of people and things like HE can. He made you that way on purpose. Part of your mission in life is to come to understand this exact point. You are HIS child. Placed on Earth to do HIS works. Yes, you are HIS servant. The more you trust HIM the more you can accomplish.

We look at this as so simple. But humans have a real hard time with all of this. Too bad!

So now you ask- this cannot be right? How am I supposed to deal with this? What am I supposed to do with this information? It is very simple.

Begin each day with a prayer. In your prayer ask God for his help and protection through the day. Or for that matter, you can ask for God's help in any specific situation. Then repeat three times with complete sincerity- I will to Thy Will! Then trust as the day enfolds. Try as best as you can to just leave all your worries, questions and every other human negative emotion behind. Like you are turning them over to God to handle. Now what better way can you get. In a way you come to view God like your loving parent and protector. Which is exactly what He wants because he is!

So, there it is- pretty simple. You might even think it is too simple. So can you explain to us –why is it so difficult for humans to do? Why is so difficult for humans to trust God.

Think about what we said when we originally started in this book. Power and control, believing in something you cannot see and trusting all become the obstacles you must overcome to enjoy this plan full in your life. That is the plan for you. Work on overcoming each one of them. But we ask you, we beg you to try. Do not give up once you reach your difficult hurdle. Think of what we are saying up to now and the ideas we share with you in the rest of this book and work your way through it. We promise if you allow yourself the chance to allow God to help you. You will not be disappointed. It is all up to you. We are just asking you to try.

In the pages that follow we are going to share with ideas, thoughts and suggestions that we help you through specific human difficulties. Because we know that the plan may seem simple but as you go through the journey of life specific concerns and problems occur in all humans lives at different times and they need extra help in getting through. So the information that follows will help each person through those difficult times.

Catherine Pagano

Chapter 4

Dealing with Life's Challenges

An Invitation

Dear Ones, A new chapter of your life has begun for you and will begin for others the moment they let go of fear. Trust that we are always with you and believe each and every day that you are guided. That makes you and all humans special. You cannot explain this or give this to anyone. It is kind of an inner knowing that has to come from the person all by themselves. They have to, in essence, want to seek it, know it, and believe. As we understand humanness will make this easy at times and hard at times. That is the challenge!

Now each of you must ask yourself –are you ready for the challenge?

If the answer is yes. We are happy because you have seen, believe, trust and will now make the commitment.

If it is no, we will guide you silently until you are ready. It is your free will that will determine how long that will be. Peace

This chapter is a series of small vignettes that are designed to help you deal with life's many challenges. In order to implement your divine plan in life, you must constantly learn to deal with life's challenges. Some are easier that others to deal with. Some are to cause great pain and are true reflections of life's crossroads. Depending on how you act or choose to act determines all the difference as to what will follow in your life.

The words placed here in the following pages are designed to get you through those difficult times while staying true to your divine plan. We hope you enjoy your life's journey and realize how close we really are to you in all that you do.

In order to complete the reading of the rest of the book, we suggest two approaches. You can read straight through it and then go back to it daily for reinforcement on key issues and words that you need at any given time. Or you can place the entire book in your hands and then let it open to the specific pages that you need at that given moment.

It really does not matter how you read the pages but what we are absolutely sure of is YOU WILL GET WHAT YOU NEED WHEN YOU NEED IT!

So enjoy the rest of your life's journey......

The Journey of Life....

The journey of life is never measured by things only actions! You can only reach as high as you think you can. That level is up to you. Be you- a unique loving individual not someone limited by people or your own thoughts.

Remove the blinders and see the real you- whole and perfect! A Child of God- just like we see a newborn precious child. Be you and live a life full of hopes, dreams, and experiences. The Grace of God is always with you. So work on not blocking it and just enjoy.

The favor of God is precious. All the goodness He brings to your life was meant to be enjoyed. Be You! We love you!

The World is changing rapidly...

The world is changing so rapidly. What people know right now will not be that way in a year from now. So one must hold onto one's core- what you believe, what matters, what is important and valued. It is from that that one will find peace and center oneself to deal with it all.

We are with you and know that you are protected. So, nothing will ever change that. Be a being of light!

Trusting God

The most difficult thing that humans must learn is to Trust God! Humans constantly think that they know better. NOT TRUE!

We function off emotions and misconceptions many times. SO... Breathe... and let go of all the fears, desires to control and conceptions we have about our lives and how it should be.

And just let God show us what He wants for us and then ... Allow Him to give it to us... Have a blessed Day!

Life's Difficulties

In the darkest hour of human despair, it is an important and curious behavior-

How humans turn to God. Not full understanding that God wants you to seek Him in all hours both good and bad. We suppose you might say that if a person turns to God in their darkest hour at least they are turning to Him and not away from Him. Yes, that is true but it is not the only time, God wants you to have Him in your life. Having God in your life on a daily basis does not mean that you are a dependent little child. It means that you understand the flow of power and energy comes from God. In a way humans exist because God so chooses. The very existence of you is linked like a fine little thread to God. This means that the very moment that God chooses your life on the Earth will end, it will. So by directly inviting God into your life on a daily ongoing basis you strengthen that thread. That pleases God.

This is not to say that you will not have difficulties in life. You will on that you can be sure. But with God in your life those difficulties will be easier to handle, on that you can be sure. So what we are promising is that if you allow God in your life on a daily basis you will develop a strong link to your creator and allow all the blessings that this life has to offer come to you.

So we are asking that as you read the rest of the book that to learn to develop within you a stronger link to your creator, Your God, the one that made you, The all-knowing. And let the divine energy come into your life, so that you may life your life to the fullest.

As you digest the rest of the book and allow it to work through you understand that you will see and feel changes within you. Sometimes those changes will be clear and sometimes they will not. Work at a pace that will feel comfortable to you. Know that some points will be difficult to accept or understand just give it time. And follow your divine plan and it will all work out. Have faith and trust!

Remember you are a work in progress! So just keep with it and watch it all enfold for you. Enjoy-

Being Put To The Test

As individuals goes through life, there are times when they are put to the test. We experience situations that cause the human spirit to question, to demand, to react, to fear, and to act. Humans find themselves full of many, many mixed emotions. Their minds race with ideas, questions, plans, and more questions.

It is a difficult time that humans truly learn the depth of their own spirit.

We are truly amazed at the depth of the human spirit during times of war. What soldiers think, feel, and react to when in situations of battle. The horrors of war demand human strength and endurance that definitely put the human spirit to the test. It changes them for life. It creates a mental and emotional comradery that is understood with just one look.

A common bond, a brotherhood which lasts for life.

This commonality gives humans a bond which can never be broken or lost- never to be forgotten. Opportunities arise to allow individuals to rise to the test. The human spirit can make a difference in some way. How interesting it would be if all humans could see and feel that connection to others. It exists but for many it is not illusive to them. It does not have to be. Humans are connected to each other through the divine. More energy needs to be places on learning just what each person's connection is and how he or she can make the difference.

In truth that is really the test that each person experiences. Rise to the higher thinking.

Make a difference. Push oneself beyond the comfort zone. The rewards are great if you only try.

How to Find Strength Through Difficult Times

There are times in life when truly difficult times come upon us and we wonder why?

Why is this happening? Why me? What did I ever do to deserve this? What am I supposed to learn from this? Am I being punished? Is God really mad at me? Will I ever survive this? Will I pass the test? Do I have strength to handle it? Am I lost? Why can't God make it all go away? What am I missing? What did I do wrong? Why don't I understand? Why? Why? Why?

Dear one- This Guide is being written to help you. Yes YOU! It is written for you- each of you to help you learn and help you realize that even in your darkest hour YOU ARE NEVER ALONE! God is with you helping you in ways you never imagined or in ways you really can't see until later. Find comfort in that. That comfort which God alone can give.

Look into your heart and mind as you read these pages and find a new awareness and a renewed strength.

Let us begin…

Ebb and Flow of Energy

There is a consistent ebb and flow of energy throughout anyone's life. So the expression "some days are better than others" is really true. The hard part is to get through the difficult days.

As humans, this is our struggle. The key is faith. Faith in God and ourselves. The message of today is to never doubt that there is God and that He is here to help.

All we have to do is keep him close to us and ask. For All things are Possible with God!

Rough Times

Life sometimes can get rough, humans always say. But it is not the roughness that is hard. It is the rigidity of one's attitude that makes it as tough as it is. Life is meant to be enjoyed. Treasured. Loved. It is meant to be a beautiful journey in which each individual learns, grows, unfolds into a beautiful flowering spirit that each one is.

NO anger, NO hatred, NO jealousy, NO frustration, NO pain! Just LOVE, LOVE, and more LOVE! Sound good? So why won't people realize it. It is all about attitude. Attitude MAKES all the difference in the world. So what is yours?

Think about it? Do you have a positive attitude? Are all the things you do out of love or just another chore? Do you see the glass half empty or half full? Check your Attitude!

Well what is it going to be…? Same old thing or something new and different? It is up to you! It makes all the difference in the world. Peace.

Surprises In Life

Surprise...Surprise... How the events of life can turn. That is what life is all about- surprises! You know that the greatest plans can all fall apart due to one change in events.

Surprise... Surprise... Humans have no control. Yet Humans think they do. How funny...!

Wait till you see what is in store for you. Things you would have never imagined. Trust, Love, Be at peace. The rest will easily for you. Go with the flow. The clearing down has emerged. You know the truth. Now live it! All will be fine. Better than you expect. Be you! The loving, giving, wonderful person you are. Peace.

Perplexed by Others

Dear One, we know you are perplexed by the way people act. They refuse to know better.

Sometimes they act this way out of fear, sometimes they act this way out of anger, but mostly they act this way out of the inner feeling that they are "unloved'-INSECURITY.

They will never admit to it but they will argue, kick, plead and fight. It is such a waste of time and energy. But how do you change someone's thinking? Unless they are ready to change and "BELIEVE" in just how much GOD loves them.

To know another human being is an honor and a gift from GOD. To love another human being is a sacred privilege that is bestowed on a person. To respect another human being is a responsibility and a courtesy. For Life is difficult enough without putting jealousy, hatred, and anger into it. So God's wish is to enjoy each other.

Dealing With Anger

Anger is a very difficult negative emotion. Most people do not fully understand its complexity. As one angers at another the interaction begin...

Harsh treatment or words are said or done; which now impacts on another person and the negative vortex begins. The spiral downward is heightens as more words or actions are said or done.

The only way to break free from this horrible cycle or negative vortex is to stop and allow the healing light to enter. From this forgiveness comes and then the cycle is broken.

For most people they cannot not get past the light entering to the forgiveness part. They think forgiveness is a sign of defeat. The dark side has cleverly masked it to humans that way. But it is not- it is actually winning!

Once forgiveness enters and is done, the person is freed from any of that negativity and light can enter more... Ultimately allowing so much more goodness to come to the person who forgives.

The key is just letting go and releasing it all... For many humans that is the real challenge. But faith can show you- it is all worth it.

Coping with Life

Dear One, it has come to our attention that we need to express a few ideas due to the nature of the circumstances in lives who read this. What is the struggle you face? Why is it such a struggle? As you focus on these questions, we ask you the following? Do you believe that God will provide?

How much do you trust?

How much do you work off the negative energies of anger, frustration, fear, worry and sadness? All of this is very human but what we are asking you to do is to have faith. You are God's child.

The Father will not let you fall... but you must let Him help you and not put the blocks to stop His love from getting to you. You set up the blocks because the negative energy consumes you and through your free will you choose to not receive the many gifts He has to offer. So you might ask- how do I get my free will not to do this? Just move it to be open to God's Love. You are in charge of your free will no one else. Think about this...

Think of the times in your life when things went so smoothly. When it all seemed to fall into place. Remember how great that felt. How happy you were.

Get yourself back to that point and begin again... Take today as the NEW day-- the Day you Begin the NEW Life you want. First- invite God into this day and everyday forward.... As you rise, begin with this invitation and thanks. Thank God for the day and all that He will provide. You can ask for things but always clarify it with the following- Lord- you know better than I- so I look forward to all that you give me today.

DO NOT get upset if it does not go the way you planned. As Long as you stay close to Him, He will show you why the day did go that way... Remember we all are part of His Plan... so cooperate... and feel blessed. Because you are! And never forget we are with you Always!

More on Life's Difficulties

In the darkest hour of human despair, it is important to note such a curious human behavior. How humans turn to God! Some turn to God with hope that in one quick motion the problem or difficulty will go away. Some turn to God in fear and say please protect me. Some turn to God in hope. Yes, Hope that God will send his angels to help. Some turn to God in anger with thoughts of why are you doing this to me? Honestly thinking God's punishing wrath is upon them or that God has abandoned them. A set of interesting perspectives…

But never forget-That God loves YOU and will NEVER abandon you. He will always show you the way. If you ask honestly and unconditionally. He will always strengthen, encourage, and guide you. Giving each person a feeling of comfort, strength, and a belief, that God really does have a plan for each of us. In this there is truth, love and peace.

Seek HIM, come to know HIM, Love HIM. With that you will learn and grow. Again Life is a journey… Always moving forward even if the steps are small. Each fit to the next, giving clarity as you go to what God's plan really is. Find strength in these words.

One of the hardest lessons of life

As humans, one of the hardest lessons of life is to learn to let go. As parents we live to nurture and raise a child to adulthood. For some the bond is simple and weak. For others it is strong and loving. Time passes quickly and it feels as if suddenly that once small child is now a grown adult ready to leave the home and move on. How scary it is for us to then be pushed into the understanding that we must let them go… We take it as a loss but it is not, in truth it is a gain. Now you might ask how so? Well look at it this way. You have raised a child with all of your ideas, values and goals. You have created another with similar purposes as yourself. As they move out into the world there is now another one of you there. You are extended. They know right from wrong because you raised them that way. They know what to do. In one way you are being asked to trust that you did your job well. Now that might be a little problem if you are unsure of that. But have no fear in a few short weeks you will know that you did a great job and now the world has two of you.. How nice - what a great gift to a parent that has done their job well. Look forward to this. Feel a sense of reward and gain for your life is now expanding. You have done a great job in being the best possible parent. Now let the universe show you "thanks". There is great reward in that. It is all a matter of how you look at it.

Human Ego

Dear One, life is a very interesting journey. Why do humans try to complicate matters by allowing their egos to get in the way?

Ego is a reflection of one's fears, insecurities and weaknesses. If you are centered in God more and more, you will find that your ego gets smaller and smaller to the point that you think more to what is right thing- the God centered thing- to do in each case than what do I want. Interesting too how one's perceptions are lost in fears and confusion when we allow ego to work or run things. But when we allow God in- all fear and confusion is eliminated. Peace and calm enter even in the most difficult of times and the person knows all is well. Peace.

Angelic Perceptions to Us

Angels speaking to us – we are always near. Yet so many choose not to ask for us. So many do not even realize. So many fears us. Why? Is it that they fear themselves? Do they see us only as angels of death? Do they fear that if God were to enter their lives now, they would not be ready? Ready? Meaning that they need to do more, say more, change more, and have not done so; thus, demonstrating feelings of unworthiness. How Human!

God sees all and knows all. He knows you need to do more. He knows all you have done. So why not accept Him actively in your life through the work of His angels. The Angels who guide you, steer you, protect you and love you! Why not? What could a human say that God does not already know? Think about it.

Finding Strength

Dear One, so many times in human lives the difficulties overwhelm people and they feel that they cannot go on. But somehow they do. God gives them the strength even when they don't know it. They are not realizing it and God will sustain them.

Please know God will sustain you now. God will provide for you now. Help is on the way. Be Still and Let HIM.

Keep Faith and Know that YOU are LOVED!

Dealing With Death….

Dear One, one of the difficult questions is about dying. Why? When? Why? Where? Why? How?

Death is a process like pregnancy. Each within their own time. Do you understand that? Many do not. The complexities of it are large but we understand. Death comes to all. Learning and going with the flow helps. But even with that lessons are learned by all.

Daily Life Challenges

Dear One, life's challenges sometimes are not in the large and difficult but in the day-to-day existence. At times you are weary and tired of the journey. If that is so, then now is the time to rest. As clarity comes; so does strength. You will see truth and know love. Then you will feel better and stronger. You are a human. You cannot do more than you have, and what is possible.

The rest is up to God. Let God in His infinite wisdom and strength guide you. Now- Let Go and Let God! Be still and know in your heart that you are loved. We are here to help. Be Peaceful. Say what needs to be say, do what needs to be done and then LOVE beyond words! It is in that love that you will find even more strength and peace to handle the day-to-day stuff.

Above all know that the angels are with you loving you through it all.

Seeing Truth

Dear One, it is an interesting thing to watch how humans see truth. They do not look at it in the same way we do.

Truth is seeing things exactly as they are. It is clear. It is real. It needs no defense. It just is. Humans may not like the Truth. But Truth does not have to be liked. It just is. The problem comes in the perception of the Truth. Humans want to manipulate truth to make it something it is not. That's where the problem comes... people rooted in truth will then see and realize how foolish hiding from the truth is. Making mistakes is part of what humans do. God knows this and is willing to forgive human poor judgments and behaviors. It is the humans that cannot forgive. How Sad! Forgiveness heals the soul. It is what allows humans to move forward and grow. Humans forget that life is a journey. One which is designed to help you learn and grow. Humans are meant to embrace the journey of life as a growing experience. For some, they have forgotten that. That is sad! One must assess the character of a person to forgive. The dark side plays on this and that is why you see so much of what is going on today.

God knows who and what each person is or is not! Those rooted in God will see Truth. Our job is to help those that cannot see. As you can see, we have much work to do. So we need you. Time is fleeting and escapes no one. Love like you have never loved before.

Searching for the Truth

Dear One, some days prove to be a challenge for your soul and free will. But we still say BE LOVING. Do not get caught up in the anger or one's ego.

Be Loving

You might question why or feel that you have questions. That is human but Searching for the truth is a difficult thing. Once you start searching for truth, you must see truth as it is. Truth is seeing things as they are without judgment. Thus, you must love things without changing them. For humans that is not easy. All to often the depth of a person's understanding of truth is based on what they will to accept, sacrifice, or for go.

What is your truth? That is the main question? Look inside you. This is the hard part for a human. One must see truth without judgment, admit error at times and be honest about one's motives and responsibilities of their actions. All too often, people will squirm, lie and walk all around this and argue that it is the truth. Expending so much energy and making it worse when truth is the easiest and safest route to take.

Trust in the Truth

The Truth needs NO DEFENSE. Be who you are and know that truth is the most important. God is there in Truth. So pray today for truth, love and the higher good. All prayers will be answered in God's time.

Loving Unconditionally

Loving someone unconditionally is the greatest human experience. Yet, for some, the confusion comes in how he or she loves. To some love means that you want to make them into what you want or think he or she should be. That is not love, it is power and control. So just accept each person and everything just as it is-Then the pressure is off from both of you. Loving then becomes so easy. Try it!

Power and Control

Dear One, we find it very interesting how humans behave. Why do they get caught up in power and control? What is gained by controlling another? Why would anyone want all that pressure? It is better to walk side by side another. It sure is "lighter". The other way is burdensome to carry all that weight and harmful to one's own wellbeing. Power and control shows such insecurity to us. It is like saying that you are afraid that this other person will not love me, leave me, work against me, or hurt me. So if I control that person I can protect myself from any of that ever happening because I will force, bully or intimidate into whatever I want. Not so at all. What it does in reality, and truth is to push them further away from you because you are not building a relationship with this person on love. In many cases it brings into your life pain and sorrow which weighs you down even more.

You must rise above this. You must look to God's light for strength. Then say I can do this. I can build relationships based on love. Once you do this you will lighten up; making everything easier and more joyous. For our view, joy is needed in world and everyone's life. The major decision is to be joyous or burdened. It is a conscious choice. So what are you deciding?

Forgiveness and Compassion

Dear One, humans need to understand forgiveness and compassion. In their ego's, they become self-absorbed and see only themselves. They wonder why everyone else isn't putting me first.

47

The karmic balance is then unbalanced. Giving and taking go hand and hand. This does not mean you give and then you take. Nor does it mean you take more than you give. Nor it is any combination of things that humans will use to justify one's actions. It all must be balanced. There is a reciprocity of energy that goes on that must stay in balance for true peace and harmony to occur.

When things are unbalanced, negativity comes in. Things are said, done and hurts develop. Humans then carry that with them throughout their lives unless they make the effort to forgive. For many the pain is so emotionally great they cannot even discuss it. They bury it deep within and never want to let it go. Now they carry it. The more they carry it the heavier it gets. Thing of the image of a two-sided scale- the more you put on one side the heavier that one side gets. Thus, the scale is lopsided. So we suggest they forgive, show compassion and let it go. Then your side of the scale is more in balance for yourself. We have seen many humans mock this approach. They refuse to do so and all we can say is this- guess you like holding to all that heavy burden and are fearful of letting go? But why? Your life would change for the better if you did let it go. No matter what reason or explanation one can offer we KNOW you would see a difference in one's life if you did. Thus by showing this compassion and forgiveness towards yourself, you forgive others, you are more in balanced.

Time to Heal

Dear One, time is needed to heal all wounds. No one human as mastered the ability to heal rapidly when there is a great deal of pain. No one will ever know how much you suffered unless you communicate it with them. The hardest part is the first words- saying what you feel or believe you feel. No one can carry the pain forever without it affecting oneself mentally, physically, or emotionally. You are no different.

So think- Act- Be loving and wise- Your Own Health depends on it. Release the stress- Let go of the pain- Be Loving and let LOVE in. For this is the essence of Who You Are.

Your Attitude

Dear One, so much depends on attitude. If a people are happy, their lives will be. If they are not, then their lives won't be. Take a look at how you look at things. What is your attitude? If you feel you worry too much, ask yourself why? What do you hope to get from it? Wasted energy!

Being responsible and practical are good things but the moment you start moving into worry, worry, worry is bad. Think about this through the day and try to catch yourself. Then remember – BE POSITIVE. We love you!

Yes, there are times when you act confused while knowing full well that everything is okay. You let your mind get the best of you. Stop. Breathe. Focus on what you need to do and not on whatever it is that getting you worried. Honestly do not let egos –yours or others- get in the way of your happiness. Do not let that shift your attitude.

Let go and let God guide you. This way your attitude remains positive, and you can do what He wants you to do. We know we will help you through everything no matter what.

You Are A Gift

Dear One, you look at the world as a series of complex problems instead of as a series of complex gifts. Gifts which are to be used and shared.

You are a gift to all those you touch; not to be used, but to be cherished. All the people in your life are to be treated in the same way. If a person treats you poorly it is because they refuse to honor you as a gift. No need to repeat their mistake and poor choice.

Separate yourself. Back Up. Ask God to forgive them and Dust their energy off and away from you. You are not responsible for their behavior. Release them to find the truth. This way you are free to find yours.

Developing Trust

Dear One, trusting others is very difficult for humans and completely understandable to us. Humans are flawed. They can lie and create situations which demonstrate to others that they should not be trusted. Free will goes in so many directions with this. There are no limits on how crazy humans behave. To us, it makes no sense. Yet on the other hand, we know it all has to do with the deserving factor- Am I worthy? Do I deserve this? And in some cases, the person's insecurities which rest deep in the subconscious say NO! So they do things to sabotage the situation and create a distrust or any other set of negative emotions. Each person has a part to play in this.

Yes, if you want trust, you must act trustworthy but for some people that is very hard to do. So, they create the drama and make it look like they need your forgiveness and even beg for it. The problem is it is something no person can give them. They must first forgive themselves- most times they don't. Thus creating a repetitive pattern which will continue until they really look at their "core" or "mindset" and change that.

Unfortunately, the people they hurt are also impacted. But there, too, understand there are lessons for both sides to learn. So now that affected person must think and assess what do I need to learn from this. So, they can move on too.

Oh what a crazy web of confusion which is sewn. Unnecessary, if humans would only act out of love in the first place. But they cannot do that based on the life lessons each person is supposed to get in this life.

Just know we are with you and will guide you if you ask.

Moving Forward

Dear One, the spirit of God is in YOU- Seek It- open your mind to it. Put the past behind you and free yourself to move forward. You alone are the only one that can.

You will never please everyone but you cannot live a life happy by not pleasing yourself. Contentment comes from knowing that you are doing the right thing. Not what others want you to do, say or be!

Your Belief in God

Dear One, what is your belief in God? At this time of year, we would like all humans to give as you call it an "attitude check".

GOD is GOD. The all, The everything! No matter what the religion it is the same. After that the different attitudes begin to break or fall apart. Why do humans do that? May we suggest, it is about power and control? Why do humans feel it necessary in their quest to connect to God that they be so possessive? Especially when they themselves do not have the power to claim ownership. God loves ALL. Everyone! All He asks is to be "His Child" focusing in just one's personal relationship with GOD. Do not worry about how others relate to him. Just you and Him is really all that exists.

We are amazed at all the lying, cheating, stealing and worse killing that is taking place on the planet under the excuse that it is in God's name. Rubbish! Wrong! Don't be ridiculous! God NEVER, NEVER, asks you to lie, cheat, steal, or kill! Never! That is where humans get confused. Do Not hide behind a "mask of God". That mask is only the devil in full force! Why cannot humans see this?

We, the Divine Messengers of God, working through a human are compelled to ask you. Please, please check your attitude! This time of year lends itself to it. So please, please consider this. Check your relationship with God NOW! Begin a new year with you growing closer to God by talking and living His Love and His Word! The planet needs you to do this. Humans need you to do this. You need to do this.

The rewards in your life are and will be so great if you do. That we can promise. You will live and feel God's love each day. You will increase your awareness of the many purposes you are to fulfill in this life time that you have been given. You will see peace enter into your life. You will realize just how much God loves you! You will learn and live the true essence of what God is "LOVE" and "Peace"- what a wonderful world this could be!

So we go back to our original question. What is your belief in God?

It does start and end with you! Peace…..

Getting Through It All

Dear One, you know it has been difficult. So many things and people all pulling on you at once. The cost is high and you never wavered- as difficult as it was- you remained steadfast in faith. Even when you weren't sure, you asked us and God for help and guidance. GOOD JOB! Though all is not over yet certain things remain at our and your attention. We wanted a chance to speak as you can see clearer.

This time it is up to you. You love with all your heart knowing full well that others do not do the same. They are blocked by their own energy and their egos. They are the ones that need the work. But you can only pray that they will grow. You can show them. You can tell them. Guide them but the rest is up to them. It is draining for you because you see their true spirit even when they cannot. The beauty of who you are is that God's faith, love and knowledge works through you.

At times in your humanness, you feel you have failed God and yourself. You have not. God knows you are human and cannot do everything-right- but you fail to realize how much you punish yourself in this process. Thinking of your imperfections as so wrong- lighten-up and move on. You were never designed or destined to do it all or be it all for another human. So let that settle in and move on.

Take time to help you look at the beauty of life; The goodness in your life, your gifts, and get back on track for you. Let us guide you to more and greater things. Lift all your boundaries and blocks. Work with the gifts and learn even more –Life and light abounds. Only you can help you. Do this now. Once you commit to this we will help you all the way. Much goodness instore for you. Let you light shine now.

We love you---Peace---- talk more later.

Catherine Pagano

Chapter 5

Manifestation is the Key

You are now ready to move on... so it begins. The most interesting thing about life is just to begin. For many they go through life by just existing- they do little, say little, have little and want it all. How funny- they look to God and everyone else to do it for them. That is not how it works. The key is just to begin. Begin life. Begin living- how? Just start with each day. No more, no less.

Consider the gift of the day as a box that you are to fill with good ideas, actions and deeds completed by the end of the day. Some days you might feel that you filled the box till it is overflowing and other days you might feel that you did not. It is not measured in human terms but in God's eyes. The key is to just begin leaving no day with an empty box. Each day matters- just begin. That is your task- your mission. Let kind words and deeds become your goal and before you know it, you will see and feel the positive energy move through you. It will bring you to new heights. You will release the old negative thoughts and hurts; helping you to heal and grow in such a smooth easy way that you will not even realize how you are being transformed into one of God's beautiful angels on Earth. It is in each human just as it is in us. It is God's hope for you in this life. The key is just to begin.

The first step is to learn very simply that thoughts, words and actions have power. While you are filling up your box each day with positive ideas, actions and deeds you must also add positive words. All this together creates images and impressions which enter into the universe. Thus you are creating an impact on what happens to you. NOTHING IS BY COINCIDENCE- THUS MANIFESTATION.

Manifestation is the process you can use to help you stay on course and work further than you even expected. Let's go further…What exactly is manifestation and why is it so impossible for so many humans to follow. To manifest you must think it, feel it and believe it is possible for you to achieve. It starts with one single idea which then keeps repeating in a person's mind. Kind of like "what I think so to I become". The more you think it you are putting energy out into the universe that this is what you want for yourself. That was why we had you start to make a list of things you were thinking about earlier. So what are you thinking and is that what you really what for yourself, If it is not then CHANGE what you are thinking! It is simple as that. Because what you are thinking impacts on your energy flow and what you attract. Everything is all connected.

How many times humans are looking for something better for themselves from the outside; failing to understand the "better" that one seeks actually comes from within. If only they would realize that if you want better- then you must manifest it in your mind, in your deeds and in your very being. You get only what you send out- so send it out. "I need more", I want this or that" are two examples. In truth you always get what you need; perhaps not actually the thing you seek. Ex. I want my freedom implies that you do not have it so you are really saying keep me without it. But if you see yourself as free it brings you more freedom-ultimately satisfying your soul's need. The same is true with fear- real or subconscious then becoming exactly what you fear. It is a shame that humans spend so much time on this and still do not get it. Happy for those that do!

Peace is not an illusion. It must be manifested from within or it never is obtained.

Chapter 6

Final Thoughts

Putting It All Together

Now as you can see the rest of your life is up to you. Follow all the instructions. Work with them daily and know that we are with you.

Each step you take in the direction of the Divine Plan will be the right one. Remembering too that there are no wrong steps. Each one will teach you something.

Learn from it and move on. If you dwell on it you carry more baggage with you to the next step. So let it go and "lighten up".

If you do nothing, you will stay stuck- so no movement takes place. When you are stuck too long you place yourself in danger of your Divine Plan coming about. So, keep moving- go forward. Any effort towards your Divine Plan is better than no effort at all.

Look to us for help to guide you here. You know by now that we will gladly. Believe in your heart that you are worthy of our help and know that with full confidence it all WILL WORK OUT!

Life is a most interesting journey for humans. We do not fully know how to explain it all to you but we have made a good effort in this book to get you started. So, you see we have made the effort- now you- as God's creation- HIS loving child- it is time for you to meet us halfway. GOD will take you and guide you from there. We have 100% full confidence in that. If you have followed our ideas set forth in this work- so do you!

So Enjoy life! Enjoy the gifts of life given to you because you are God's child worthy of no less. Be still and take all that in.

Breathe in an out so slowly and truly absorb that thought

Is it not wonderful? Is it not amazing? Is it not the best positive morale booster?

Nothing is better. YOU are God's Child- worthy of the best and nothing less. So enjoy life!

On your way to true fulfillment remember these few things. On a daily basis. Follow your Divine Plan- Remember- Not my will but God's will be done!

Take every moment every day to live following that. Look for guidance and know that you are being directed. Even if difficulties arise know that with God's help all things are possible. So do your best to never let negative energy get in your way and allow it to block all the goodness you are entitled to have in this life.

Trust This!

Is it not wonderful? Now knowing what you know. If you go back to our first remarks in the beginning of this book and re-read them. Can you understand our confusion?

Knowing what you know now. Why would anyone opt for something different? Truly you can see here the work of the evil one has unfortunately corrupted human thinking.

But HAVE NO FEAR! It is time for you, each of you, to know!

That KNOWING what you know now and following your divine plan- You can turn your life around! The past is the past. Forget it! Leave it like you would your old toys. You learned from them at one point in your life but now you must move on taking that knowledge and using it to get to a much "Higher" "lighter" place.

Do you know how ridiculous you would look to other humans if you started playing with your old toys now? They would ask questions like- Why are you playing with children's toys? Why haven't you thrown those toys out? What you even still have them? Why?

They will always be fond memories in your mind but a child plays and does child things. A grown-up has other things. It is not the same. You can't take them with you. You must let go.

So in a way this book is most definitely about you doing some mental and physical house cleaning. All for the purpose of getting your house in order; for the better we might add.

Is it not comforting to know this? It should be. And If it is not comforting with you then... there are areas that still need cleaning. So continue on. Follow your plan and it will come to you in the right order.

Several points to consider

Do Not frustrate yourself by trying to move too fast or hold onto something too long. In either case it will not work or help matters at all. Realize that if everything is in proper sequence all will run smooth. If you hit "bumps", "blocks", or "hurdles", ask yourself why? What are you doing to cause this? Then trust the answer you get even if it is not an answer you like. No matter what the answer, do your best to follow it. For if you try to change it, you will only give yourself more problems in the end.

Now you might ask- "How will I know I am getting the "Right" information as an answer when I ask?" This is simple- just ask the question 3 different times (same question now). If the answer is still the same- rest assured, it is the right answer.

We give you this technique for the human skeptics. For those that truly believe you will know on the first round, so you won't even waste your time asking twice more. Given time even the skeptic will be convinced. Just follow your divine plan. It is really that simple.

Now let us also explain that even the best of humans will have their "moments of challenge" when you will be tested to see if you truly get it. Why and when we cannot say. Just know it has to do with your life's evolution to the higher plane level and your karmic mission. This means that within each lifetime you serve there is a different or lesser theme. Depending on which one you have, your moments of challenge will be to see if you have learned the lesson or are you following the theme. There are too many individual variables to take time within this book to explain. But just realize if you follow the steps, we have outlined for you in this book, knowledge will come the more you trust. The more you trust the more knowledge you get; and so on and so on.

This is one of the best and most beautiful levels of human understanding when you finally feel connected to the universe and that at your disposal is all of the universal knowledge you need at any given moment in time. Sure, would feel good and comforting- so why not have this in your life? You can!! It is just that easy- just follow the steps given.

Now we know that you are a little skeptic. Still inside of you- you are going to ask- If it that easy how come thousands or millions of people have not discovered this before?

They have in their own way throughout time. How else do you think great ideas, inventions, technology and happenings have taken place. Just on pure human thought alone? Do not be ridiculous. Not by coincidence remember! Add to this- why now? Why you? That is easy. Because You are ready and You need it in your life NOW. It really is that simple. Pretty Impressive? We think so and now we hope you do too!

Chapter 7

Summation

We have chosen in this book to conclude with an informative summation which we have divided into four parts.

Part I - About Us

As you have read this book in its entirety we gave you very little information about who "we" are. We refer to ourselves as the foursome. To tell you now is that we represent the four Archangels- Gabriel, Michael, Raphael and Uriel – for the most part- This is who we are. But we also represent every other level of Angels in the Universe. We "friendly four" are easy for you to identify with and relate to so please do so and continue to do so. But throughout this book it really did not matter which one of us was talking more. We truly represent God's wishes here- so call on us as you wish.

Part II –About The Book

This book is the first in a series of four books which will be written. This one is focusing on introducing you to the endless possibilities of the universe and how you as a human connect to it. Realizing that this is the introduction may be new and even difficult to grasp. We wanted to make it a "LIGHT" reading. Pun intended here. We don't want to frighten you away. We wanted you to get a feel for us and how the universe works. And how you can improve your relationship with GOD, yourself, and others. Thus further moving you down the spiritual journey of life.

The other three books which will follow will deepen your enlightenment and offer you endless other possibilities. Each to be written in an order which you will understand and written when you are ready to experience it.

Remember Do Not use human time in this. It will be universal time.

Let this book envelope your life. Once you and the ideas of this book are completely one then the next book will arrive. "Nothing by Coincidence."

Part III- About the Writer

Ever since she was a little girl, we have watched over her. She is our chosen one to write for us. This is her true mission among so many small missions she has been given.

Why her?

Because despite the many adversities she has faced in life she has never, never, given up or lost her faith. Since she was small, she prayed and believed in saying thanks for the many gifts she was given even when to others it may not have looked like a gift.

She spends countless amounts of time putting others above herself- serving and loving to serve. And she has worked on trying to find a spiritual balance, growth and development. Above all, since her awareness evolved about her own "gift". We found her very easy to talk and through her. She is a very special lady! If you ever meet her- you will say the same thing too!

She is real and understands the human spirit well. For this we realized our choice was easy as to why her. You can learn more personal information on her at the end of this book itself.

Part IV- Why NOW

Why after so many thousands of years have we chosen to write now? That is easy- It is time!

As the new century enfolds the focus of humankind must change. Based on history, humans have done many wonderful positive things. Yet, they also have done many terrible ones. Of late it seems that in many parts of the world, the world is off center. This book is designed to remind humans that you are not all powerful and that harmony and cooperation should be the focus-not power and control.

The Earth is a gift to you. It is home but a gift for you to care for, share and improve on- not destroy. As we look at the planet, we see more and more destruction. Of course, we realize it is wrong and really a slow means of self-destruction. Because if you destroy the Earth, you are destroying yourself. Eventually one leads to the other. Everything is connected remember!

So, we felt that we must speak out to get the attention of humans. It will be the single efforts of each individual that will combine to help save the whole. Each individual matters. What you do counts. NEVER think that you have no impact on the Earth-You Do!

So, we wanted to call your attention to all of this by starting with helping YOU! Now we think you can understand where we are going with the future writings. First you must establish harmony and peace in your own life before you can see beyond that to global consequences. So now you understand our purpose of this first book.

We believe that by applying the principles established here- you are well on your way to enlightenment. We are glad for you. The world truly is a much better place when you "lighten" up.

So grow, learn and enjoy. Knowing full well that life is a beautiful journey and that you do have an intrical part in it all!

Your presence does matter! You are special and unique. So trust.

Be still and know that I am.

Catherine Pagano

Chapter 8

About the Author

Cathy Pagano was born and raised in Paterson, NJ. Growing up in a close knit loving Italian family in a poor neighborhood, she learned to value the small things in life. Since her mother's family all were very religious, she experienced all the traditions and rituals of the Roman Catholic faith. Praying and talking to God was a normal everyday occurrence. Being thankful for everything was instilled in her by her mom, dad, aunts and grandparents. When she was 10 she lost her maternal grandparents and aunt all within six months of each other. The family life changed but the faith got stronger in different ways.

As Cathy reached high school, she developed an interest in education. Her parents insisted that she go to college but could not afford much. Starting at 16, she worked and helped pay her way through college. She achieved a BA in History and then a MA in Urban Studies from Montclair State University. She realized she loved teaching and pursued a long and wonderful career as a high school teacher. She taught US History, AP US History, and Sociology. She developed innovative programs for students and till this day loves working with young people. Although retired after 44 years, Cathy remains active as a consultant to the school by working with the students on various patriotic and community service events.

A key life changing experience occurred as her mom was preparing to pass away in 1984. Cathy and her mom were blessed with the visitation of an Angel "Carol" to help her through that very difficult week. Little did she realize just how that week would change her life in so many ways. Since was a graduate of the Silva Method in 1981, she worked through her daily meditations. She learned how to grow closer to God and the Angels. She became aware of things that no one else knew. She learned to understand humans and seek God and the Angels for so many things in her life. She started helping all those that came to her and knew her life was about serving others.

As she accepted more and more of what God's plan was, the journey got harder. The dark side continually pushed and challenged her to stop and move away from what God wants her to do. So, there were times that she would stop and not continue onward in the development of this book. It has been a journey but we knew all along that she would finish it.

So, we hope she will act as an inspiration to you to keep pushing on. We know you can complete whatever your mission is.

Chapter 9

Angel Message Cards

Based on the writings of this book, these Angel Message cards were created to help you through your daily life. There are many ways in which you can use them. You may wish to pick one each day. You may only want to select one when you feel you need it. It is up to you.

Here are a few suggestions whenever you do use them.

- Sit quietly. Meditate if possible first.

- Have the book open in front of you to where the cards begin or you can make copies of the cards and keep them separate for yourself. Ask the Angels to provide you with whatever insight you need NOW. Then as you hold them let the Angels guide you to the ones you need.

- Then, in either case, let yourself gravitate to the card or cards that you need. You will get some information, clues, or direction to help you at that given time.

- If you want you can even keep a journal to record the experiences to help you the more you keep working with your Angels!

May you find peace, inner strength and happiness as you go! God's Love and light to you!

****

Hope and Pray:

Overcoming pressure is not easy.
Knowing what is right,
wanting to do "good",
and facing the daily challenges which involve
others can be stressful.
Just remember you can hope and pray.
God will hear your prays and help you to find a balance and a
solution even in the darkest hours!
So Peace and patience are needed now!

Be Love,
Show Love

**Things can change.
Just relax, have fun and do the best that you can do.
Somethings you cannot change but with love you can help
others to find ways to change.
Life is interesting, go with the flow-
just Be- LOVE and Show- LOVE**

Travel Wisely

Many tasks of life are not easy.
Each one is unique to the individual.
Sometimes we expect others to be and think like us.
They may not be able to do that.
So learn to just love freely and unconditionally.
This way you will be traveling in life's journey enjoying the
simple pleasures.

Just Be

Each Human being is a unique creation of God!
No need to compare at any level.
Just BE.
Travel your own path.
Your lessons are just for you- no need to compare!
Just Be!

Planting Seeds

In life we find individuals that are not moving forward.
You want to help.
But sometimes the best that you can do is to plant seeds of
thought and allow the person to develop it so as to grow like a
flower!
Who knows maybe you can see some sees planted within you as
well.

Focus On Your Needs

As a human you need some retreat time to focus on your needs.
Give yourself a chance to process.
Access the entire situation and figure out what is best for you.
Until then-Silence is the best here.

Just Relax

**Just be Still-
Cleanse the body and the mind of all negative thinking.
Work on this for a few days and you will see improvements.**

Finding Balance is the Key

Balance is a big key in life.
Taking time for you is most essential!
Your body and mind needs it.
Strength comes once you do.
So use your time wisely
and do not demand too much from yourself.

Serving Others
is the
Highest Task in Life

**Accepting a mission to serve others in any capacity can be
difficult. It is filled with many complications.
But it can be rewarding and joyous in many ways.
Keep your perspective and know
you are doing God's work on Earth!**

Be Silent- Do Not Give up Your Power

**There are times in life that being silent is the best.
When dealing with difficult people who are not listening.
Arguments only lead to you losing or giving up your power.
Do not go there-
Be silent!**

Be Alert and Look for the Signs

**Change is a part of life.
It is not to be feared but it may not always be easy.
But one thing for sure something good will come from it.
So look for the signs and await the better days!**

Do Not Be Afraid

Fear can make you stuck.
Do not do that to yourself.
Know that the Angels are always working with you,
so invite them in and trust that good things are in store for you.

Better Days are Coming

**Remember sometimes it has to get worse before it gets better.
Stay focused and hopeful.
Things are working in your favor
even if you do not feel or see it.**

The Path Is Clear

Do Not be afraid to pursue what is Truth.
Truth should never be feared.
It maybe layered and take time to unravel all the layers. Just let it unfold.

Stay Positive and Let In The Light!

**Remember – Letting Go is Letting God handle it.
Direct it to HIM.
Strength and Love are your assets –
So- Stay Positive and Let in God's Light!**

Use Your Free Will for Good

**You have a choice-
Free Will is God's Gift to you.
You can choose to be negative-angry, fearful or
You can chose love, happiness and peace.
Look at every situation and make your choice**

Keep Your Promises to Yourself

At times you must examine
the promises you have made to yourself.
Are you working to keep them or not?
Re-examine them with love and patience then move forward to
keep them.

Stop trying to change things which cannot be changed

Somethings in life are not for you to change.
Let Go!
No reason to get upset and focus on what you can do.

Be Hopeful

**Some days bring pain and sorrow.
But New brighter tomorrows are ahead.
So focus on the future and Be Hopeful!**

Keep Busy, Be Positive and Smile

**You are a wonderful person!
Use your wisdom to move forward
because better days are ahead.
SO SMILE!**

Show Love,
Be Love

**Be Free to Be Who You Are-
A Beautiful Child of God!
Show Love and Be Love to all,
knowing God is with You!**

Never Give Up Your Power

**NO matter how others may try to manipulate you,
Never give up your power.
Time, Friendship, and Truth are all important
but are never to be used to impose on someone.
So remain true to who you are.**

Be Love
Know Love

**There is a giving and a receiving to Love.
Very often humans think one must continually
give love without opening their heart to receive Love.
Open your heart today**

Be Aware of the Forces Around You

**Remember, the dark side
would love to win you over
to the negative.
That is not going to happen.
Just stay focused and rooted in love.**

Express Truth

It is hard for humans to understand or accept truth sometimes.
Time will tell if they do.
It is up to them.
Just know-It is what it is- truth.
When spoken with love
it may be necessary to say or hear.

Be Calm Show Love

**Throughout your daily routines,
be calm and show love each day.
Everything will take of itself
knowing that you are centered
in such a peaceful place.**

Just Breathe,
Be Still,
and Strength will come

**Focusing on your own stillness and breathing
you will find the strength and calmness to achieve much.
Make this part of your daily routine.**

Take Time for You today!

Smile, Pray, Be Happy!
Center yourself today
on things that bring happiness and truth.
Do what you need to do
and distance yourself from negative distractions.
Feeling better will be your goal today.

Stay Focused on the Truth

**Truth is your theme especially today.
Be calm. Do what you think and Know is right.
Stay focused on Truth, you will remain calm.
Then more positive energy comes your way
instead of getting caught up
in the negativity of the world around you.**

Peace is a State of Mind

The feeling of Peace is the time when you are most connected to God! If you seek it, you are seeking God in your life. It is a commitment you make with God to keep that connection even when humans can make it impossible. You are invited to seek Peace! Just remember- With God All things are POSSIBLE!

Be Kind,
Be Calm,
Be Patient,
Find Balance

Humans can give you a million and one reasons not to be.
God is asking you to look beyond all the humanness
and do "good" anyway.
Doing what is right
will bring you balance and peace!

Patience and Time are with you. No need to seek control

**All too often Humans seek
to control a situation or person.
When in truth they control NOTHING!
GOD is in control!
Put your trust in that just let God handle it.
You then gain the wisdom that
time and patience are on your side.**

Be Still

There are times in human life when
the best thing that you can do is to Be Still.
Do nothing.
Let the situation play itself out.
Praying instead to invite God
into the situation and let Him handle it.
Then just Be Still!

Find Your Mission

In the journey of human life,
each person has at least one mission
if not many more.
Have you found yours?
If yes,
Are you fulfilling it to the best of your ability? I
f no,
What are you doing to find it?
You should always be working on a mission in life.
SO breathe in, ask and trust the answers.
Then start moving.

Postscript

It is my sincerest wish that this book will help you on your life's journey.

Never forget that God and the Angels are always with you.

Catherine Pagano

Catherine Pagano is available for interviews and personal appearances. For more information contact us at info@advbooks.com

To purchase additional copies of these books, visit our bookstore at:
www.advbookstore.com

"we bring dreams to life"™
www.advbookstore.com